BACKYARD SAFARI

Ants

Trudi Strain Trueit

Cavendish Square

New York

Published in 2014 by Cavendish Square Publishing, LLC
303 Park Avenue South, Suite 1247, New York, NY 10010

Copyright © 2014 by Cavendish Square Publishing, LLC

First Edition

Website: cavendishsq.com

This publication represents the opinions and views of the author based on his or her personal experience, knowledge, and research. The information in this book serves as a general guide only. The author and publisher have used their best efforts in preparing this book and disclaim liability rising directly or indirectly from the use and application of this book.

CPSIA Compliance Information: Batch #WS13CSQ

All websites were available and accurate when this book was sent to press.

Library of Congress Cataloging-in-Publication Data

Trueit, Trudi Strain.
Ants / Trudi Strain Trueit.
p. cm. — (Backyard safari)
Includes bibliographical references and index.
Summary: "Identify specific ants. Explore their behavior, life cycle, mating habits, geographical location, anatomy, enemies, and defenses"—Provided by publisher.
ISBN 978-1-60870-240-4 (hardcover) ISBN 978-1-62712-026-5 (paperback) ISBN 978-1-60870-816-1 (ebook)
1. Ants—Juvenile literature. I. Title.
QL568.F7T57 2013
595.79'6—dc23
2011020699

Editor: Christine Florie
Art Director: Anahid Hamparian
Series Designer: Alicia Mikles

Expert Reader: Christina Kwapich, graduate student research fellow, Florida State University, Department of Biological Science

Photo research by Marybeth Kavanagh

Cover photo by Mark Moffett/Minden Pictures
The photographs in this book are used by permission and through the courtesy of: *SuperStock*: age fotostock, 4, 8; Minden Pictures, 6, 7 (top), 7 (bottom), 15, 22TL, 22TR; IndexStock, 23TR; AnimalsAnimals, 26; *John C. Abbott/Abbott Nature Photography*: 10; *Getty Images*: Visuals Unlimited, Inc./Alex Wild, 11, 25; *Alamy*: Medeni, 14; Rolf Nussbaumer Photography, 22LR; John Cancalosi, 23TL; *Newscom*: Colin Hawkins, 16; *National Geographic Stock*: Moffett/Minden Pictures, 18; *Visuals Unlimited, Inc.*: Alex Wild, 21, 22LL, 23LL; *Corbis*: Alex Wild/Visuals Unlimited, 23LR; *Landov*: A. Skonieczny/DPA, 28; *Media Bakery*: Veer, 13 (brushes); BigStockPhoto, 12 (baseball cap), 12 (sunglasses); *Cutcaster*: Marek Kosmal, 13 (magnifying glass); Sergej Razvodovskij, 13 (pencils)

Printed in the United States of America

Contents

Introduction

Have you ever watched baby spiders hatch from a silky egg sac? Or seen a butterfly sip nectar from a flower? If you have, you know how wonderful it is to discover nature for yourself. Each book in the Backyard Safari series takes you step-by-step on an easy outdoor adventure, then helps you identify the animals you've found. You'll also learn ways to attract, observe, and protect these valuable creatures. As you read, be on the lookout for the Safari Tips and Trek Talk facts sprinkled throughout the book. Ready? The fun starts just steps from your back door!

ONE
Amazing Ants

Ants may be tiny creatures, but they are hardy. Ants have lived on Earth for more than 120 million years. These insects once walked with dinosaurs! Ants are also among the world's most plentiful animals. For every person in the world, scientists estimate there are at least one million ants! Ants may be found marching across snowy forests, sandy beaches, hot jungles, and even the floor of your house.

Trek Talk
Scientists have identified more than nine thousand kinds of ants on Earth but figure there are another ten thousand types they have yet to discover!

Ants live in **colonies**. A colony may be made up of a handful of ants or millions of them. Most colonies **nest** in warm, dark places, such as under soil or rocks or in rotting wood. Each colony is built around one

Worker fire ants take care of their queen and her pupa.

or more queens. The queen starts the colony and is the only female within it that can have **offspring**. Most of her children are females that cannot reproduce. They are known as worker ants. Each ant has a job. The queen's job is to lay eggs. The worker ants (the queen's daughters) do everything else. They look after their mother and her young, dig tunnels, remove trash, protect the nest from enemies, and find and store food. As workers age, their jobs change. The first job a worker ant, typically, holds is in the nursery, and her final job is either finding food or defending the nest. Some of the queen's children are males and new queens. These ants are unique, because they are the only ones to develop wings. These winged offspring will soon fly away to mate with ants from other colonies. After returning from their mating flights, the males die. Young queens shed their wings, begin nesting, and form new colonies.

These are new queens and male imported fire ants. All of them have wings that they will soon shed.

Nature's Farmers

Leaf-cutting ants use their strong jaws to slice the leaves off plants. They cut the leaves into pieces, which they then carry back to the nest. Each ant carts a leaf piece up to thirty times her own body weight; that's like you hauling a car in your teeth! Leaf-cutters don't eat the leaves they collect. Instead they use them to grow a type of **fungus**, or mold they feed on. The rotting leaves provide nutrients for the fungus crop to grow. A queen starting a colony will take a bit of the old fungus with her to start a new fungus garden. She carries it in a special pouch in her mouth. In North America, leaf-cutters are found mainly the southern United States. A single leaf-cutter colony may have more than 5 million ants!

An Ant's Life

An ant egg is about the size of the period at the end of this sentence. A newborn ant is a **larva**. It is a simple creature without legs, wings, or antennae. It looks like a grain of rice. The larva's job is to eat and grow. Worker ants carefully look after each larva, feeding and cleaning it. After about a week, a larva reaches full size. It may spin a **cocoon** (kuh-KOON) to pupate, or change into an adult. Not all larvae spin cocoons. Some simply lie quietly in the nest. The **pupa** (PEW-puh) looks very much like an adult ant, but is white and inactive. During the next two weeks the pupa changes. It develops a **thorax**, an abdomen, and a head. It grows legs and antennae. Males and queens will form wings. Just like butterflies, ants emerge from their cocoons as adults. Worker ants join their sisters in the colony, while queens and males fly away to mate. Queens will then start new colonies. When the queen dies, the whole colony is usually doomed, for there are no other females to lay eggs.

These are harvester ants during their pupa stage of development.

Trek Talk
A queen ant may live up to fifteen years and produce 150 million daughters during her lifetime!

Ant Anatomy

Ants belong to an order of insects called Hymenoptera (Hy-men-OP-tera). It means "membrane wings." This group of insects also includes bees and wasps. Like their buzzing cousins, queens and male ants have wings. Remember, worker ants do not have wings. Many types of ants have something else in common with bees and wasps: stingers. Only female ants, bees, and wasps can sting you. Stingers are actually modified egg-laying tubes. Female workers can't reproduce, so over a long period of time their egg-laying tubes evolved into a defensive weapon. Males don't lay eggs, so they don't have stingers!

Like all other insects, ants have six legs and three main body parts: the head, the thorax, and the abdomen. A thin waist, which connects the thorax to the abdomen, is what sets ants apart from other insects. Another distinctive feature is their bent antennae. Ants use antennae for taste, touch, smell, and communicating with other ants. Did you ever wonder why ants often seem to play follow the leader? One way ants "talk" to each other is by releasing different chemicals, or **pheromones** (FARE-uh-moans). Each chemical sends out a different message, like "danger, go back!" or "follow me, I've found food!" Ants use pheromones to make a trail to and from food, mark territory, mate, and attack or flee from enemies.

Ants have two sets of jaws. The outer jaws are called **mandibles**. These jaws are lined with sharp teeth and are used for heavy-duty tasks like cutting, digging, and fighting. The **maxillae**, or inner jaws, are comblike and are used for cleaning and chewing food to release liquids. Ants eat only liquids. They may mix digestive juices with seeds, dead insects, or fungus to turn them into liquid before eating them. Some ants prefer **honeydew**, a sugary liquid released by aphids (AY-fids), leafhoppers, and other small insects. The ants tend their aphids the way humans look after cattle. They "milk" them, build shelters for them, and even move them inside during the winter! Ants also have an extra storage-stomach called a crop. Ants can share liquid food from the crop with their sisters.

Now that you've learned more about how ants eat, live, and work it's time to see them for yourself!

Ants belong to the same group of insects as bees and wasps. They share common body parts as those of other insects.

TWO

You Are the Explorer

While on safari, you may spot an ant dragging a seed across the driveway. Or discover a line of ants heading back to the nest with all kinds of treasures. It's also possible you might not see much at all. That's okay. An ant safari takes time, patience, and a little luck. You'll improve your chances of success if you choose a day when the temperature is above 50 degrees and it isn't raining. Take a friend along, you're sure to have fun!

Trek Talk
Ants can lift up to fifty times their body weight!

What Do I Wear?

* A hat with a brim
* A long-sleeved shirt
* Jeans or long pants
* Sunglasses
* Sunscreen

What Do I Take?

* Digital camera
* Magnifying glass
* Small paintbrush
* Plastic spoon
* Small plastic container
* Notebook
* Colored pens or pencils
* Water

Trek Talk

Slave-raiding ants invade the nests of other ants, stealing larvae and pupae to raise as their own. After they are born, the kidnapped ants don't even know they've been stolen. They live and work alongside their captors.

Where Do I Go?

Ants like to nest in warm, dark places. To find them, look for these things in your backyard:

* Fallen trees
* Tree stumps
* Log piles
* Concrete patio or driveway
* Piles of leaves, grass, bark, mulch, or dirt
* Flat rocks, loose paver stones, or stepping-stones

Tree stumps are a great place to begin your ant safari.

If your backyard doesn't offer these features, here are some other good safari locations:

- ❇ Meadows
- ❇ Woodlands
- ❇ Fields
- ❇ Beach
- ❇ Public parks

Always have an adult with you if you are going beyond your backyard.

On the March

Army ants get their name from the way they swarm across the ground like military troops. These night hunters overwhelm, kill, and eat the insects they meet. Army ants have no permanent nest. Instead, they make a nest out of their own bodies by hooking their legs together in cavities. They take shelter each day under leaves or rocks. In this photograph army ant workers form a bridge along a trail for colony members to cross. They are found mainly in the midwestern and southern United States. Look for groups of army ants on sidewalks and paths as the sun begins to set. They move quickly but are rarely a threat to humans.

What Do I Do?

✲ Use your magnifying glass to search for ants marching across the grass, a deck, or a concrete patio. When you spot an ant, follow it to see where it goes.

✲ Look for signs of an ant colony. Remember, ants dig tunnels to make their nests. Some go as far as 35 feet under the ground! Ants remove the dirt or wood from their tunnels, which they pile up outside the nest. Do you see a small mound of sawdust near a tree stump? How about a little pile of dirt or leaves in the flower garden? An ant nest may be nearby. Also, check under flat rocks, loose paver stones, or stepping-stones. Ants especially like nesting in these places. Stones absorb heat from the sun, which keeps the nest warm.

A magnifying glass is a handy tool to use when searching for ants.

- ❋ If you find a nest, do not touch it. Some types of ants will attack when threatened. Acrobat ants may bite, while fire and harvester ants may sting. Keep a few feet away from any nest you find. Sit quietly and watch how the ants behave.

- ❋ Take notes on your discoveries. What color are the ants? Do any have wings? Where did you find them? What are they doing? Look at what they are carrying or how they are using their antennae for clues. Snap a photo or make a sketch of the insects you find.

- ❋ As you make notes, leave a line on the bottom of each entry for the type of ant (you may be able to fill that in later).

- ❋ Make a drawing of your insect beside its entry or leave space to paste in a photo.

ANT

Color(s): rusty red (no wings)

Location: on cement step on back porch

Activity: two ants carrying a large

insect wing

Insect name: _____

Your Drawing or
Photo Goes Here

* If you want, gently scoot an ant onto the spoon with your paintbrush. It's best not to touch ants, because some may sting or bite. Place the ant in the plastic container you brought. Use your magnifying glass to get a better look. Does the ant have wings? If so, it is a male or a queen. If not, it's a female worker ant. Most of the ants you'll find will likely be female workers.

Safari Tip

Your magnifying glass will give you a great close-up view of an ant's most important sensor: its antennae. Watch how these tiny stems are in almost constant motion—tapping the ground for a scent trail, waving in the air to check the temperature, or touching another ant to communicate (right).

* After a few minutes, let the ant go. Place it back where you found it so that it can rejoin its colony.
* Spend about a half-hour to an hour on safari (don't forget to drink your water).
* Clean up the area and take everything with you when you leave.

Now that your safari is over, did you get some great photos or see something amazing? Congratulations! If not, don't worry. Make plans to go on another safari soon. No two expeditions are ever alike. Next time, you will see and experience different things.

At home, download your photos onto the computer and print them. Get your photos and notebook. Move on to the next chapter. It's time to learn more about your backyard visitors!

THREE

A Guide to Ants

You've had a busy day trekking through your backyard jungle. Now you're ready to try to identify the ants you've discovered. Here's how to do it.

Compare your photos, drawings, and notes with the ants on the following pages. As you do, answer these questions:

* What is the main color of the ant? Typically, North American ants are brown, black, or rusty red. They may also be a combination of colors. An ant may have, say, a red head and thorax and a black abdomen.
* What is the ant's texture? Is its abdomen smooth? Does it have ridges or hair?
* Does any particular feature stand out? Perhaps the ant has a large head or long abdomen.
* How did the ant behave? Did it spend most of its time on the concrete? Was it carrying a leaf (a leaf-cutter ant, perhaps?) or a seed (a harvester ant)?

Once you've identified your insect, go back and write its name in your notebook. If you took photographs paste them in your notebook, too.

ANT

Color(s): rusty red (no wings)

Location: on cement step on back porch

Activity: two ants carrying a large insect wing

Insect name: pavement ant

If you're having trouble making a match, don't worry. There are more than seventy types of ants common to North America and hundreds more that are not so common. That's far too many insects to picture here. Also, remember there are thousands of types of ants on Earth that are still unidentified. Who knows? Perhaps you have discovered a new species!

Ant Guide

Army Ant

Leaf-cutter Ant

Acrobat Ant

Red Harvester Ant

Ant Guide

Honeypot Ant

Black Carpenter Ant

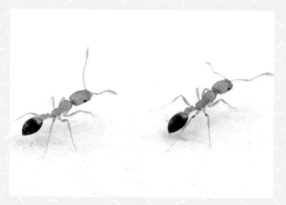

Pharaoh's Ant

Odorous House Ant

FOUR

Try This!
Projects You Can Do

People often consider ants to be pests, especially when colonies nest in homes and buildings. Even so, ants are very good for the planet. They do many important things. As they dig their tunnels and build nests, ants bring air, nutrients, and water to the soil. Ants move seeds so that new plants can grow. They spread pollen, too, giving us flowers, fruits, and vegetables. Ants are good recyclers. They eat dead plants, insects, and other animals. They also eat living things, such as caterpillars, beetles, and grasshoppers. Without ants, these insects would feast on the food that farmers grow for humans. Groups of army ants may also help to drive away larger pests, such as mice and snakes (though they, typically, don't feed on them). Ants are also food for other animals, including anteaters, armadillos, and birds. Many types of North American woodpeckers eat ants as their main food source. Woodpeckers use their long, sharp beaks to drill into trees and stumps to find them. Here are some fun projects you can do to learn more about these helpful insects.

That Full Feeling

Honeypot ants are living food-storage tanks. Some members of the colony, called **repletes**, fill their bellies with nectar and honeydew. They get so bloated they can barely walk! The ants hang upside down in the nest (if they fall they can burst). When food is scarce, the repletes share their stored liquids with the rest of the colony. In some parts of the world, people eat honeypot ants as a sweet treat!

Ant Picnic

Ants aren't picky eaters. They'll go for just about anything from meat to fruit to cereal. Give the ants in your backyard a mini picnic while you learn about the foods they like best. Place an index card near where ants are living or working. Put a sugar cube, a corn-flake, a strawberry, and cookie crumbs in a line on the card. Wait for some ants to find the card. Which food do the ants go to first? Do they seem

Ants love sugar! Here they enjoy the sweetness of a piece of candy.

to like one food more than another? Hint: Ants prefer sugar. Write in your notebook about what you see. When you are done, don't forget to throw away the card and food.

Follow the Leader

As you've learned, ants use pheromones, or natural chemicals, to communicate with each other. An ant may leave a scent trail to tell other ants where it has found food. You can see ant pheromones in action with this simple project. All you need is a small paper plate, some honey, and a large leaf. Place the plate near where ants can be found (on a patio or the grass). Put a few drops of honey on the plate and wait for ants to find it. Once a line of ants is heading to the honey, place the leaf between two ants in line. How do the ants react? What happens when you take the leaf away? Write down your observations in your notebook. Scientists have also discovered ants will often use landmarks to help them find their way home. With an unbroken line of ants heading to the plate of honey, make a small change to the environment. Perhaps, hold a small branch above the plate or move a rock that's nearby. How does changing the landscape affect the ants' behavior? Take notes about what you observe. Be sure to throw away the plate of honey when you, and the ants, are finished.

Trek Talk
Ants use up to twenty types of pheromones to "talk" to each other.

Ant Drinking Station

Ants drink dew, or water, from grass and leaves. It's easy to make a drinking station for ants on a hot day. Cut a standard kitchen sponge into quarters. Soak the quarters in cold water (you can add a bit of sugar to the water, too). Place the sponges outside near where ants live or work. Watch to see if the sponges attract ants. You might get a few or, if you're lucky, a whole line of thirsty ants! Be sure to bring in the sponges at the end of the afternoon.

An ant is about one-millionth the size of a human! So it hardly seems possible that people and ants have anything in common. Yet the truth is we share many personality characteristics. Like ants, we live in tight-knit communities. We work hard. We protect our homes. We value our families. Maybe that is why people find ants so fascinating. The more we learn about them, the more we understand ourselves.

Common black ants drink a drop of water. Try creating a drinking station for the ants in your backyard.

Glossary

cocoon   a silky covering spun by insects to protect them while they pupate

colony   a group of organisms

fungus   an organism, like mold, that lives off the nutrients it absorbs from decomposing matter

honeydew   a sweet liquid secreted by aphids, leafhoppers, and other small insects

larva   the feeding and growing stage of a young insect

mandibles   an ant's strong outer jaws used for fighting, digging, and other difficult tasks

maxillae   an ant's comblike inner jaws, used for cleaning and feeding

nest   a place where insects lay eggs and raise their young

offspring   children

pheromones   chemicals released by ants that allow them to communicate with each other

pupa   an insect in a nonfeeding, inactive stage as it changes from larva to adult

repletes   honeypot worker ants that store liquid food in their bodies for the colony

thorax   the middle section of an ant's body between the head and abdomen

Find Out More

Books

Gallagher, Debbie. *Ants* (Mighty Minibeasts). New York: Marshall Cavendish Benchmark, 2012.

Stewart, Melissa. *Ants*. Washington, D.C.: National Geographic, 2010.

Woodward, John, Stephen Moss, and Nicholas Forder. *Insects*. San Diego, CA: Silver Dolphin Books, 2010.

DVDs

Ants: Little Creatures Who Run the World, WGBH Boston Video, 2007.

Master of the Killer Ants, WGBH Boston Video, 2008.

Websites

National Geographic for Kids

http://kids.nationalgeographic.com/kids

Here you can read about the fascinating lives and habits of ants. See insect videos, including those of the leaf-cutting ants in action, and play games, too.

The Oakland Zoo

www.oaklandzoo.org/animalsarthropods

Log on to explore the social lives of honeypot ants, leaf-cutters, and other amazing insects.

PestWorld for Kids

www.pestworldforkids.org/ants.html

Did you know odorous house ants give off a smell similar to that of coconuts? Discover more interesting facts about the ants that may be living in your backyard at this educational site.

Index

Page numbers in **boldface** are illustrations.

About the Author

TRUDI STRAIN TRUEIT is an award-winning television weather forecaster and news reporter. She has written more than seventy nonfiction books for children on everything from storm chasing to video gaming. She is the author of nine other books in the Backyard Safari series, including *Squirrels*, *Spiders*, *Caterpillars and Butterflies*, and *Beetles*. Trudi lives near Seattle, Washington, with her husband, Bill, a high school photography teacher. Read more about her at www.truditrueit.com.